PURSUIT

FREEDOM

BE YOURSELF, INCREASE YOUR REFERRALS AND HAVE MORE FUN GROWING YOUR BUSINESS!

ERIN BRADLEY

Printed in the United States of America

Pursuing Freedom, 2016

Pursuing Freedom Publishing
PO Box 1150
Winter Park, CO 80482

Ordering Information:
Quantity sales. Special discounts are available on quantity purchases by corporations, associations, and others. For details, contact the publisher at the address above.

www.PursuingFreedom.co

Table of Contents

Intro

Congratulations on being your own boss! You are a driven and passionate person, inspired to design your life and create your own destiny. And like me, you are probably realizing just how hard that journey can be! You know you are good at your craft, but generating business and maintaining a consistent income is easier said than done. You plug away and work hard, but financial security remains elusive. Well, my new friend, I commend you for picking up this book. I applaud you for investing in your future! It shows you haven't given up, and you shouldn't! The road to success can be much easier, and much more fun, than you've ever imagined. So buckle up and enjoy the ride!

Let's face it. "Sales" and self-promotion can be brutal. The majority of entrepreneurs don't become self-employed because they were born salespeople. They start their own business or go 100% commission because they love what they do, and they're good at it. They don't want a boss telling them how to do it, when to do it, or where to do it. They want to be free to do it their own way. They follow their passion, sacrifice the steady paycheck, and get to work. But for many, the idea of picking up the phone to share the good word, and 'sell' their product or service, is terrifying. The thought of keeping in touch with past customers and potential referral partners is scary, because they don't want to bother people. They don't want to be seen as 'salesy.' But the fact of the matter is: in order to make a living doing what you love, you've got to figure out how to sell it.

This book is going to change your perspective on what it takes to make sales, and help you make more money doing what you love, so you can enjoy the freedom you were seeking to begin with. This quick read will provide you a simple, easy-to-follow strategy to multiply your business and have fun doing it.

Like many people, I became 100% commission in the pursuit of 'freedom.' I envisioned a life of travel, working when I wanted, where I wanted. I was hardworking, but free-spirited. I longed for success but feared being tied down. I was on a mission to avoid the "9 to 5" and pursue financial freedom *my way*! There was just one problem. I lacked a very important skill, and that was the ability to promote my services in a way that would create a consistent and sustainable income. In other words, I spent the first several years flat broke. I was still having a blast, but my bank account was not.

It took me hitting financial rock bottom before I realized something had to give. I became hungry for knowledge, obsessed with finding the link between 'free' and 'financially free.' I devoured books, hired business coaches, and attended seminars trying to find something I could latch onto and apply to my business. I needed to find a plan that would work, and one that would feel good too. The strategies in this book are a result of years of study and practice. My goal is to help you succeed, and faster than you ever imagined possible.

This book is going to provide you a replicable system for growing your business by referral. The 'scripts' I'll provide you are not your traditional (and often dreadful) sales scripts. This strategy is about changing the conversation. It's about communicating your message in a way that's authentically you, and adding value for your audience. It's about building a village of people you love, who love and support you right back. I've taught this business model to realtors, financial planners, hairdressers, massage therapists, electricians, and more. The principles are applicable to anyone trying to grow their business by referral, and the system makes the process purposeful and fun.

If you're still in doubt, let me tell you Talia's story. In early 2013, she was 26, had recently moved to Colorado, and had started her business as a photographer. In speaking with Talia about how she was marketing her business, she informed me that most of her clients found her online. When I asked her if she was keeping in touch with her clients in order to build referral business, I saw her cringe. What could she possibly have to say to her past clients that would warrant her keeping in touch with a phone call? She didn't want to bother anyone. When I showed her my system for keeping in touch and providing value beyond the 'closing' of the sale, she found an approach that she could identify with.

Since then, I've seen her take the lead on a number of proactive campaigns, collaborating with like-minded entrepreneurs to provide more value for her clients long beyond the photo shoot. And this approach has led her to multiply her sphere, and continuously earn referrals from the clients and colleagues she loves the most. And I'm pretty sure she's having fun doing it!

I can promise that if you take the advice in this book, and apply the principles to your own business, you will see your results multiply. You will be working with people you like. You will be better connected with your friends, clients, and colleagues. And both you and your bank account will be happier than ever before. Don't let your fears prevent you from living the life of your dreams. You started this journey in the pursuit of freedom, just like me. And that's exactly what you deserve. But you can't be free while stressed about money. No more wondering where your business is headed or how you're going to 'find' more clients. This book is about creating your destiny, and sharing your joy with every person you meet. Take action today and start making a bigger impact doing what you love! Enjoy the journey.

CHAPTER 1

Have you ever been BROKE?

et's start at the beginning. Ground zero, where most entrepreneurs start out, is a scary place. In the summer of 2008, I was broke. I'd been 100% commission as a mortgage broker for exactly 10 months, and I was so broke, I had to ride my bike to a first time meeting with a client because I didn't have enough money for gas. The Starbucks was 5 miles from my house, so I showed up early to wipe the sweat off before my client arrived. Since it was my first time meeting him, I had to make a good impression. Well, let's face it; I was desperate and needed the business.

So I walked up to the counter, ordered my tall black coffee (who could afford a latte?), handed the barista one of my credit cards, and crossed my fingers. Declined. And who walked up, right as my card was being declined? Yup, Mr. New Client and Next Paycheck, who also happened to arrive inconveniently early for our first appointment. So what does one do? I could try one of my other maxed cards, in the hopes there was $2.10 available *somewhere*, but if another card was declined in front of Mr. Paycheck, how would I explain THAT? So I did the first thing that came to mind. I lied. "Huh, that's odd. That's my debit card, and there's definitely money there. Hmm, shoot, it's the only card I have on me." So Mr. Client bought my cup of coffee as I stood there mortified. I had officially hit my version of financial rock bottom. Heck, I know it could have been worse. I mean, at least I had a bike. But one doesn't take being declined for a $2 cup of coffee easily. Something had to give.

So I did the first thing that came to mind. I called someone who could surely give me some advice on the situation: my dad. When my parents were somewhere around having their second of five children, my dad decided to change career paths and go the route of 100% commission income as a stock broker. He quit his job as an engineer, commuted from Cleveland to Pittsburgh 4 days a week to get his MBA, and ultimately went into sales. So I asked him, "Dad, how did you get started with 100% commission income? I mean, how did you survive?!" To this day, I'll never forget his response. He said, "Well, you weren't alive yet (I'm #5), but we had bill collectors calling, the electricity shut off, you name it." "So what did you do?" I replied. "Listen Erin," he said, "do you think you're going to be good at this?" I thought about it, and yes, I did. So I told him so, with conviction. "Then you do whatever it takes." So I did.

The next day, I opened another credit card (EEK!!!!), bought Internet leads, and kept plugging along. (I also received a $2,000 check in the mail and a note that said, "Pay me back when you can." Which, of course, I did... thank you, Dad!) I changed companies, invested in coaching, and literally did whatever it takes. The only issue was, while I was spending money I didn't have on coffee meetings, lunches, marketing, and leads, I still didn't really have a plan!

This is a common theme I see time and again with anyone trying to grow their business. There is just SO MUCH we 'can' be doing to grow our business, but what actually works? And is it even enjoyable? Or are we "doing whatever it takes," whether we like it or not, because frankly, we're starving for a paycheck? And when the paycheck comes, how many will it take to reverse the damage we've done? In my case, it took years. So believe me when I say you have to do whatever it takes. My only hope is that you apply your perpetual energy to a strategy that will work, and save yourself the years of stress and debt it took me to figure it out.

Did I mention I was engaged to be married at the time? You know, that fun, magical, exciting time, when you spend your summer shopping for the perfect veil, the shoes, the right necklace for the big day? Yeah... the following month, my husband and I flew from Colorado to Pennsylvania for the big day, and packed in one carry-on bag. For both of us. For a 3-week trip that included getting married and a honeymoon in Maui. You read that right. We packed in 1 carry-on bag. And I forgot to pack shoes for my wedding day. Well, I claimed I'd forgotten.

Everyone laughed at the flighty, free-spirited youngest child. Who packs for a 3-week trip that includes their wedding, and shares a carry-on with her fiancé? And who forgets shoes for their wedding day?! The truth is, the shoes cost more than that cup of Starbucks coffee. I'm not sure how we managed to get flights home for the wedding! They must have approved me for another credit card, seeing what a perfect candidate I was for not paying it back.

At this point, you're probably thinking one of two things. If you've been in my shoes (or currently don't have enough money for shoes), you're probably nodding your head in understanding. And if you haven't, you're probably wondering how a well-educated college graduate gets into a predicament like this. And better yet, who is she to be writing a book that would bring you any value?

The thing is, I *knew* I was going to be successful; like most people who become self-employed, or accept 100% commission income, I *believed in myself.* I just didn't know the why or the how. Not only did I have no idea how one builds a business from scratch with no training, I had no money to start with! So I was winging it. And what I've learned over the past 8 years is that I'm not an island here. For the purpose of this book, we're going to consider 'self-employed' and '100% commission' one and the same. Both are wired with an entrepreneurial spirit, a nagging sense that something better exists for us. We won't be bound by a boss or a salary! We're worth more than that! We may technically be an employee of a company, perhaps an independent contractor, but we're entrepreneurs at heart, freedom seekers committed to creating our own financial destiny.

So why do so many of us end up broke and in debt? And how do we get out from under it? How do we keep that fiery spirit alive, the spark that got us going, when we're stressed about how we're going to pay the bills? Or better yet, how we're going to buy the plane tickets home for the holidays, make it to our sister's wedding, the college reunion, and all the fun things that make life worth living? We gave up the security of the salary for the reward of freedom and money, and now we're just trying to get by. And the life of the footloose and fancy free, as it turns out, is really freakin' expensive!

The challenge many of us face is that we took the risk without a game plan for success. I jumped ship for the life of freedom without a safety net. But I'm here to show you the system that finally took me from broke to 6 figures, all without selling my soul to the devil.

Much of what I've learned, and what you'll learn from this book, is a compilation of ideas I picked up from coaches, books and colleagues over the years. I just found the ones that resonated with me, latched on, made them my own, and molded them into something that is authentically me. So just know, some of this stuff will work for your business, and some of it won't. Whatever clicks, run with it! With reckless abandon, take a few critical ideas, make them your own, and watch your results soar.

As I mentioned, we are going to begin at ground zero. We are going to start with our 'why.' In the next chapter, we are going to walk through the process of identifying your goals. If you've been in business a while, you've probably done some business planning and goal setting, because, well, it's the smart thing to do. On the other hand, you might be just like me. The unfortunate side effect of being an impulsive and spontaneous person is that goal setting seems pointless. Who knows what the future holds?! Why would I be bound to a PLAN? And even if I wrote out a plan, I can't control the outcome anyway!

Well, friend, I'm here to tell you that I made the sad mistake of being in business for 5 years before writing out a business plan, and we now know how well that worked out for me. So let go of your inhibitions, and let's dive right in.

I always wonder why
birds stay
in the same place
when they can fly
anywhere on the earth.
Then I ask myself
the same question.

— Harun Yahya

CHAPTER 2

Start with the End in Mind

Before you can make a plan to grow and improve your business, you need to have goals. I didn't set any goals for the first 5 years of my business. I've never been a planner. I've always just assumed things will magically work out in the end. I'm the kid who forgets to pack sunblock for an African safari in the desert. I'm the mom who forgets her kid's homework project, not at home, but in the mountains an hour away. It's a combination of scatter-brained and free spirited... two characteristics that don't lend well to business planning!

I never felt I had any control over my results, so why set myself up for disappointment? I was growing my business 'organically' or 'by accident,' as they say. I was winging it. I just assumed if I plugged away long enough, success would be inevitable... someday. If you're wondering how this approach worked out for me financially, see the previous chapter. Not so well! Don't get me wrong, my belief that "all will work out in the end" has been immensely helpful in staying the course all these years. It just wasn't too effective when it came to creating a consistent and predictable income.

"Learn to expect, not to doubt. In so doing, you bring everything into the realm of possibility."
— Dr. Norman Vincent Peale

Setting goals and writing them down is absolutely critical to your success, and should be step 1 in getting you from where you are to where you want to be. Once I started writing out my goals, I miraculously started hitting them! And it was fun! So I started setting bigger ones. And guess what? I'm still hitting them. There's actually no limit to what you're capable of. You just have to take the time to dream big. This book isn't about goal setting, but there's no point in reading further if you haven't taken steps to create a plan, a target. It was probably my most critical mistake in the early years of my career. It most likely stemmed from fear and self-doubt. What I've learned is, it doesn't matter if the dream seems unattainable at first. Once you write it down, put some focus on it, and leave it in sight… the universe begins to align to deliver it to you.

"Entrepreneurship is a state of mind, a can-do attitude, a capacity to focus on a vision and work toward it."
— Barry Rogstad

I will never forget the first time someone convinced me to start mapping out a vision for my business. It was 2011, and I signed up for a 5-week course with Darylle Dennis, founder of Inspired Action, LLC. At the time, we were deep in debt for the second time. Our first child was less than a year old, and over the course of the previous year, my income had gone down by about $35,000 while our spending had remained the same. Ironically, we were about $35,000 in debt. Funny how that happens!

I remember Darylle walking us through a goal-setting process. She advised us to put ourselves in a positive state of mind, and then mentally drop in our life goals. One of the gals in the class raised her hand and asked, "How does one put themselves in a positive state of mind when you're stressed about how you're going to pay the rent?" So Darylle walked us through a short exercise. First, she had us take a piece of paper, and write a number that represented a business goal. The number could be a target income, a number of closings, a number of clients, whatever was appropriate for us and our industry. She then asked us to close our eyes and bring to mind the happiest day of our lives. She told us to feel the sand in our toes, hear the music, feel the breeze, remember the smell, etc. We sat there for a few minutes, marinating in the joyful memory. And then she told us to drop in our life goal. Just drop in the number as you're sitting there re-living the bliss of your happiest moment. Lastly, she handed out a piece of paper with the following quote, which to this day is hanging in my home:

Until one is committed, there is hesitancy, the chance to draw back, always ineffectiveness concerning all acts of initiative and creation. There is one elementary truth, the ignorance of which kills countless ideas and splendid plans; that the moment one definitely commits oneself, then providence moves too. All sorts of things occur to help one that would never otherwise have occurred. A whole stream of events issues from the decision raising in one's favor all manner of unforeseen events, meetings, and material assistance which no one could have dreamed would have come their way.

Whatever you can do or dream you can, begin it. Boldness has genius, power, and magic in it. Begin it now!"
— Johann Wolfgang von Goethe

I wrote two numbers that day. One was for a target number of closings per month, and one was for a target annual income. It took me exactly one year to hit the target number of closings (so I wrote a bigger number!). And it took me 4 years to hit the target annual income. It was a lofty goal, but you know what, I did it! I wrote the number, kept it in my mind's eye, and went to work on the strategy I'm about to share with you.

By December of 2014, it was becoming apparent that setting goals was an integral first step to actually hitting those goals. I had even written a business plan for 2014, and had seen some great results! So as I reflected on the year, and looked ahead to 2015, I took it a step further and simplified my process into a one-page business plan. You can see a copy of it on page 93. I met with my accountability group (learn more about the power of accountability groups in Chapter 6) to share our business plans, and mine was a laugh.

By this point, the guys in my group knew me well. They joked that not only could I not plan a year out, I couldn't plan next week. So the fact that I made a color-coded one-page plan, while some of theirs were 15 pages or more, was pretty hilarious. It was like a kindergarten version of a grown up's business plan. But you know what? It's now 2016, and when I look back on that plan, I can honestly tell you I hit every major goal. The only challenge I had, and continue to have, was sticking to a fixed daily schedule. Staying present with my schedule, and not reacting to everything that comes at me on a daily basis, is a constant struggle, but it's worth working towards! The bottom line is this: magic happens when you set goals and put intention behind your efforts!

So before you read another chapter, write your goals. See page 86 or visit http://www.pursuingfreedom.co/business-planning-worksheet/ for a step-by-step process I use every year to arrive at my business plan. It's an organic process that walks you through a year in review, and draws out the highlights, the struggles, and the areas for improvement. As you work through it, you'll find your goals start jumping off the page. You'll identify your strengths and weakness, and you'll know what you need to focus on to improve and hit those goals.

If you don't take the time to work through this and create a thorough business plan, at least write a number. And if you have to, sit and ruminate on your favorite memory before you do. Get yourself into a positive state. BELIEVE anything is possible. Don't worry about how you're going to get there. Just dream big, and write it down. Then let's get to work.

CHAPTER 3

Who do you WANT to do business with?

Another fundamental of your business plan is deciding who you want to do business with. One of the greatest books I've ever read is called *The Go Giver* by Bob Burg and John David Mann. It was given to me as a gift in 2011, which was right around the time my business started taking off. The basic concept is that success comes from intending to give more value than you ever hope to receive in payment. When your focus each day is to serve others, your days are more joyous and your business is more profitable. Some may think it's hokey, but the law of attraction really does work. As soon as you stop worrying about what people will think of you, and start thinking about how you're going to help them, your fears will wash away.

Before you can start giving value, you have to decide WHO you want to do business with. And not just who you want your clients to be, but who you want your referral partners to be. This is your Village. This is your community, and will be the foundation for every action step you take to grow your business going forward. I'm not just referring to your 'target market.' I mean, who do you *like* spending time with? Building your business plan around serving people you enjoy is the first step in making your job fun.

So create an Excel spreadsheet, or just grab a pen and paper, and start making a list of everyone you know, and I mean every single person you like, who likes you back. If you're just getting started, this will be friends and family. And before you say you don't know enough people, open your Facebook account, and add every person you are friends with on Facebook (provided you like them!). If you've been in business for a while, think about past clients, colleagues, referral partners, etc. Take your time, and really think outside the box. Don't forget your kids' teachers, your doctors, your neighbors, etc. Don't worry what you're going to do with this list, and don't leave anyone off. This is a really important part of the process, and the foundation for success.

The next step is to organize the list. This is why I like an Excel spreadsheet to start. It can be a living document that changes over time as people move up and down on your list. When I finally started taking my business seriously, I signed up for a fantastic coaching program called Buffini & Company. They provide a great system for sorting your database, and even have a website and mobile app to help you keep it organized and accessible.

One of the things I've always struggled with is sales for the sake of sales. This is an odd thing to explain. Any book you read is going to tell you that sales calls are an integral part of growing a referral business. But when working on my database, even when I know I'm looking at a list of people who *like* me, I freeze up the minute I consider picking up the phone. I would have no problem reaching out to a friend to wish them a happy birthday or see how they're doing. But if I'm calling because I'm working on my business, the anxiety sets in. For so many of us, this is where the roadblock occurs. We don't want to 'bother' people, and the reason this feeling wells up in us is because at the end of the day, it still feels like we are picking up the phone to serve ourselves.

Obviously, we are trying to grow our business. We wouldn't invest all this time and energy into reading a book about growing our business if we weren't looking to increase sales and the bottom line. It can just be really *hard* to take action with our business in mind. So what I would suggest when building your village is to simply organize the list with love in your heart. In other words, put your favorite people at the top, the folks you know well and would pick up the phone and say hi to without batting an eye. When you're getting started, don't worry about the next step, just have fun with it. But do remember, this is a business strategy. If your business is like mine, and localized to a certain region, this list should include people in the market you're serving. In other words, if you're licensed in New York, you don't need to include your cousins who live in California. Once you've got your list, and it's organized, you're ready to get started. And you will succeed even if there are only 50 people on the list.

In the next chapter, we're going to dive into the process behind systematically building a referral business around people you love. It all starts with identifying your Village, which you've done. Now comes the fun stuff!

CHAPTER 4

Build your Tribe

Now that you've established the Village you're going to serve, your number one focus is to provide value, above and beyond the product or service you're selling. You're going to put all your energy into finding out their issues and solving their problems. This is where the fun begins. If you are an electrician, and your friend needs to hire a home inspector, it would be great if you could refer them to someone amazing. This means, you need to know an amazing home inspector. If you're an insurance agent, and your client wants to buy a new home, they need a good real estate agent. How cool would it be if you could refer them one? In order to be this resource to your friends, family, and clients, you'll need to set out on a mission to build a Tribe of amazing colleagues who can help you better serve your Village.

More than anything else, you are going to become the most well-known connector anyone has ever met. Your Village is going to think of you as their Yellow Pages. They're going to call you with questions, text you for referrals, and spread your name around town as the person who has all the answers. And referrals for *your* business are going to start flying in!

Why? Because once people are talking about you, relying on you to be their resource for just about everything, referrals are going to come as a byproduct. When someone is in need of YOUR services, you'll be top of mind. If John Doe called you yesterday to ask you for the name of a good landscaper, and today, their neighbor Jane mentions she's in need *your* services, John is going to immediately refer you without hesitation. Not because you've been doing a great job *selling*, but because you're a human being who cares about people, and people appreciate you and care right back. They are going to *want* to help you. It's the law of reciprocity. You're top of mind because you've kept in touch, and because you're providing value. It's a sales strategy that doesn't feel salesy!

In my business as a mortgage consultant, my clients typically only need my services once every few years. And frankly, when they don't need a mortgage, they rarely care about being kept up to date with the latest mortgage news. I've always joked that mortgages aren't sexy, so I've got to find a way to stay exciting to my clients long beyond the loan closing. And this comes in the form of being a resource, caring about their problems, and making an effort to solve them. When I talk to my friends and clients, I don't market myself as "Erin, the Mortgage Lady." I market myself as Erin, the lady who's "got a guy" for everything. And I tell them, "When you need a mortgage, I've got a guy for that too...but I'm 'the guy!'"

In this chapter, I'm going to provide a very easy to follow system for building your Tribe, and earning more referrals by default. Step 1 is to print off the worksheet found on my website www.pursuingfreedom.co.

You can also find a copy on page 94, although I prefer having it printed and on my desk daily, as a physical reminder of what needs to get done. Your first mission is to fill this list with trusted local service providers you can refer business to. Begin by filling in the blanks with anyone you already know, like, and trust. This is critical. ONLY put them on the list if you can refer them with unwavering confidence. Ideally, they know, like, and trust you back. But don't get hung up on that... we'll get to building that trust in the coming chapters. Once you've filled in the sections you can, you are likely to have at least a few categories still empty. That's okay. In fact, if your page is nearly blank, it means there is that much more opportunity out there!

Now it's time to get to work. I have found that the best way to build my Tribe is to ask my Village for help. I'm going to provide you a script that I've used time and again... any time I've felt I need to give my business a jumpstart. (Sorry to say, but lead generation isn't a one-time gig, so yes, I've used this system numerous times, and every single time, I've had huge results!) This is where you get into activity. This is the lead generation system for the anti-salesperson in us. This isn't about selling your product or service; it's about communicating your value.

Before we get started, I want to reiterate, this is a business development system, so it should be targeted, and it should be specific to your business. So before you start, pick 3-5 categories from the http://www.pursuingfreedom.co/build-your-tribe/ that would make great power partners for your business. In other words, if you're a financial advisor, you may pick the accountant, the estate planner, the mortgage banker, and the insurance agent. If you're a massage therapist, you may want to connect with chiropractors, acupuncturists, physical therapists, and personal trainers. For the purpose of this exercise, which is getting started, it's okay to be hyper focused.

So identify a few categories that would be integral relationships for your business, and we're going to start there.

Now that you have your small target list, you're going to call every single person in your Village, and ask them if they know anyone who works in these industries. Here's your script:

(_____)? This is Erin, how are you? Hey, I was just calling with a random question for you. You know how I got into the real estate business last year? Well, part of my business plan for 2016 is to grow my business referral directory. My goal is to be a resource above and beyond the real estate closing. I really want everyone to think of me as their yellow pages, and call me when they need anything, not just real estate. That said... I was wondering, since you're (<u>an accountant</u>), you might happen to know a good (<u>financial planner</u>)?

> (Let them answer while you take notes, or have them text you the contact.)

Awesome, thank you! And is everything good with you? What's new? How's work, how's school, how are the kids, any travel planned for this year, etc? (*** **see note below***** try to leave with an 'action item.') Glad to hear it. Well if you ever need a referral for a service provider, please think of me, and if anyone you care about has any real estate questions, you know I'm always happy to help! If they're anything like you, I'm sure I'd love to work with them!

A few things have happened in this brief conversation. First of all, congratulations, because you just made your 'sales call!' But your message wasn't about sales, it was about providing value. In one short call, you communicated your intention to be a resource, offered to help with something in their personal life, and reminded them you are always growing your business. A critical part of this conversation is to go deeper... *ask* what's going on with them. If you make the call too short and hang up, you miss an opportunity to PROVE your value.

I read an amazing book called *The 7 Levels of Communication*. In it, Michael Maher encourages you to leave every call and meeting with an action item. I love this for a few reasons. One, it forces you to listen better, and be more present in every conversation and meeting. And two, it provides an opportunity for you to demonstrate your intention to be a resource, by following up with something that will help the other person. You leave the call or meeting with a reason to send a note, include a business card of someone that can help them, and if you don't have someone to refer them to, it inspires you to find someone! And if you think about it, there's a snowball effect here.

A client asks me for an HVAC company, and I don't have one, so I reach out to a few realtors and a builder I know, and I ask them for a trusted referral. I reach out to their referrals, learn a bit about their business, and determine who would be a fit to refer my client to. I circle back to the client, provide value, give business to a respected HVAC company, make contact with a few target referral partners (the realtors and the builder), all while opening the opportunity to connect with other like-minded business owners in the community (the HVAC companies).

I can then follow up with a 'thank you' note to the realtor who referred the HVAC company, including my business card, and reminding *them* to think of me if any of their clients ever need a referral, or if they have mortgage questions. I can follow up with a note to the client to say it was great chatting, and include the contact for the HVAC company. And I can set an appointment to meet the HVAC owner. That's a LOT of activity! And guess what... it has nothing to do with mortgages. I'm busy, I'm on purpose, and I'm in contact with people who influence my business, but not once do I feel the anxiety I felt when trying to do 'sales calls' in my early days.

Here's an example of how this has worked for me in the past. I call a client to see if they have a good accountant, and I find out they are having a baby. I get off the phone and immediately call their realtor to let her know, and now she has a reason to reach out to the clients and make contact to congratulate them. The realtor and I have the opportunity to catch up and discuss potential business opportunities. Then, I send a congratulatory card to the clients, and include a gift card to Babies R Us, along with the business card of my favorite newborn photographer. Not long after, the clients contact me about buying a bigger house, and refer me some friends of theirs who are buying their first place. Both the realtor and I have new business, the clients feel cared about, and relationships have deepened.

Then the clients end up using the photographer for their newborn photos. The photographer also buys a house, uses me for their financing, and refers future newborn, wedding, and family clients... ironically, her clients tend to be great clients for me, as they are getting married or growing their families and often need to buy a new home. True story.

Here's another example. I contact someone in my Village, making my calls to grow my Tribe, and find out one of my clients is looking for a new job. Turns out a colleague of mine is hiring, so I connect them. My colleague's business grows with the addition of this new team member, my referrals increase, and my client is able to buy or refinance thanks to their new job. This has actually happened on more than one occasion.

Taking it a step further, there are times when providing value means *not* earning the business. There are going to be times in your career when someone wants to hire you, and you're not the best person for the job. Rather than simply decline them and leave it at that, it's important to take it a step further and try to help them find a solution. In other words, seek out someone who *can* help them, and be that trusted referral source again. The positive ripple effect for your business can be astonishing.

Let me elaborate. Not long after I started using this system, a friend of mine became accustomed to texting me for referrals for service providers. She already owned a home, and came to know that I had a lot of resources for local contractors. Then one day, she reached out and asked if I could help her refinance. As it turns out, my company at the time wasn't able to do her loan. Rather than give her the bad news and leave it at that, I researched a few local banks, and found one who could help her. She was able to refinance and save quite a bit of money. Despite not having done the loan myself, she was grateful for the direction and began referring business my way. To this day, I can easily count more than 30 transactions over the past few years that came to me as a result of a referral from my friend. The bottom line is: operate with an intention to help people. Don't worry about what you're going to get in return. Just treat people with love, and know it will come back tenfold.

It's all about changing the conversation. You are doing nothing more than connecting with people you care about, asking them to help you build your Tribe, so you can better serve your Village, all the while building your own business by default. There's something magnetic that happens when you simply strive to be of value. It's so much easier! And you know what's even more amazing? Those folks in your Tribe, who you've been referring business to, adding value to their lives... they become your clients too. Before you know it, your Tribe is part of your Village. And it's one big happy family. Your business can be a total love fest! I kid you not.

In *The 7 Levels of Communication*, the book I love that I mentioned before, Michael Maher talks about "call anxiety." He says if you're having trouble picking up the phone to call past clients, it's because you're thinking too much about yourself. As soon as you pick up the phone with the intention to get to the bottom of something going on in *their* life, it takes the focus off you and onto them, and makes it really easy to reach out and help. As human beings we are wired to want to serve others. Make this your mission and watch your business explode.

In the next chapter, we are going to dive in a little deeper, and take this whole process to the next level. The best part about this system is there's no end in sight. And as long as you stay focused and have some fun doing it, you truly cannot fail!

CHAPTER 5

Now what?

If you've taken action and filled your list by getting on the phone to your Village, it's likely you're already seeing more referrals coming in. I found there's a magic to it. I can't make 20 calls without getting a referral. And it's not always direct from the conversation... it's more to do with the law of attraction. I set my goals, get into activity, and things just start happening. As I mentioned, I've taught this system to a number of entrepreneurs in different industries. And if they follow the script, and get into action, they start seeing results immediately. When they don't, I can usually identify why.

There are a few common issues I see when folks are just getting started with this system. First off, as simple as it may sound, if you're not used to making calls to friends and past clients with the intention of growing your business, it may not come easy. The fear will still be there for a while in the beginning. Someone once told me that the more you step outside your comfort zone, the bigger your comfort zone will grow. So just know this may be uncomfortable at first. It was for me. But I am here to tell you, it gets easier. And it starts to be really fun!

So the first mistake I see folks make is forgetting to get to the action item. In other words, we get trigger happy. We make a list of 10 people we are going to call today. We know which "Tribe member" we're asking them to refer to us. We pick up the phone, make the call, ask the quick question, say thanks, and get off the phone. PHEW! We made the call! But we forgot to go a little deeper.

It's okay to make baby steps. Heck, you made a sales call! But remember, we want to *demonstrate* our intention to be of value. So rather than just letting our Village know we're building this Tribe to serve them better, we need to *show* them how we're going to do it. Getting to the action item is the most important part of the call or meeting. It gives us the excuse to follow up. I would recommend before you pick up the phone to make your calls, just write on a piece of paper, steps 1, 2, 3 and 4.

- Step 1: explain that as part of your business plan, you've decided to build a business referral directory of trusted local service providers. Your goal is to be a resource, above and beyond what you do for a living (be sure to mention your profession - that's your plug!).

- Step 2: Let them know there's a gap in your directory, and ask them if they can refer you a great (Tribe member) that they love. If the answer is yes, jot down the contact info. If the answer is no, make a note. This will be one of your action items. Once you finally fill the gap in the directory, you'll be able to follow up with anyone who expressed they didn't have someone they use for that service, and proactively pass out a referral!

- Step 3: ask them a few questions about what's going on in *their* life, professionally, personally, or recreationally.

- Step 4: thank them and remind them to think of you any time they need anything, and if anyone they care about has questions about your business. Be sure to follow up with a handwritten note!

This brings me to another common issue I've seen, which is the failure to follow up. Every single time you speak to someone on the phone, you have an opportunity to write a note to follow up. And likely, you have an opportunity to make a few more calls. If they expressed a need, they are looking for a pediatrician, an electrician, a hairdresser, you have an opportunity to not only refer them someone in your Tribe, you also have an opportunity to reach out to that Tribe member and let them know you're sending someone their way. And when you make this call, follow the 4-step process again!

Let's look at another example of how this could work. Let's say you are an insurance agent, and you are starting to make your calls, and your first call is to your friend Katie. And let's assume Katie is a massage therapist, so you call her and ask her if she knows a good chiropractor, and she recommends Dr. Ben Smith. You happen to know Katie bought a new house a few months back, so after thanking her for the chiropractor contact, you ask her how it's going with the new house. She gives a general response of, "We're loving it!" You (*proactively*) remind her that if she ever needs referrals for any projects around the house, she can think of you. She says, "Actually, I have been looking for a good electrician. We want to install some ceiling fans this summer." You say, "Oh, for sure. I know an awesome one. His name is Chad Brown. I will text you his contact."

The first thing you do when you get off the phone is text Katie the contact info for Chad. Then, you write a handwritten note, letting her know it was awesome catching up, include your business card, and a reminder she should let you know if you can ever be a resource to her, or anyone she cares about, in the future.

Next, you call Chad. You let him know you're sending your friend Katie his way. Then you follow the 4-step program. "Hey, while I have you on the phone, I'm sure I've told you that part of my business plan as an insurance agent is to market myself to my clients as the yellow pages, and I noticed I'm missing a good home inspector. I thought since you're an electrician, you may know of a good one?" Take down the info, and then ask him what's going on his life, personally, professionally, or recreationally. See if you can find out a need that would allow you to provide *him* some kind of resource. At the end, remind him "If you or anyone you care about ever has questions about their insurance, you know I'd love to be a resource." After you hang up, send him a handwritten note, thanking him for taking such great care of all your clients, including your card, and reminding him to think of you as a resource in the future!

At the end of these two conversations, you've got a chiropractor and a home inspector you can reach out to and set coffees with. When you go for coffee, go with the intention to get to the bottom of what's going on in *their life*. Find a way to be of value. Maybe you can teach them this system and help *them* grow their business. Heck, maybe they need a review of their insurance plan, and you've just picked up a new client! Or at the very least, maybe you'll make a new friend, a new person for your Village, *and* a new member of your Tribe!

This is where things get interesting. You've spent some time making some calls, building your Tribe. Your list is growing, and you're feeling on fire with all the things you've been able to do to help your Village. In fact, your business is probably suddenly really busy! And if it's not busy enough, let's take a look at your Tribe. There's a whole lot of opportunity waiting right there!

How many of the business owners on the list know, like, and trust you? How many are referring business to *you*? If the answer is 'very few', how do we change that? This is about creating a love fest between you, your clients, and your colleagues, so that everyone is benefiting. It's time to start really getting to know these people, especially because I wouldn't refer someone with confidence without ever having met them. So you start by setting appointments with the Tribe. Again, it's okay to start with the ideal power partners... ideally you have a few to meet within each category so you can weed out the duds and find the ones that are in alignment with you! Here's your script for setting appointments:

Is this _____? Hi there, my name is Erin Bradley, and I'm calling because we have a friend/client in common. (Name) says are you are pretty fantastic, so I just wanted to touch base with you. The reason for my call is that I'm in the (mortgage) business, and part of my business plan has always been to market myself as a resource to my clients, above and beyond the (loan closing). I basically market myself as their Yellow Pages, so they think of me when they need just about anything. Anyway, I was talking to _____ and mentioned I needed a good

(_____) to add to my referral directory and she recommended we connect. If you have time, I'd love to grab a quick coffee, and learn more about you and your business. When I refer people to my friends and clients, I like to make sure I've at least met them and gotten to know them. If you'd be interested, I have some availability next Tuesday or Thursday before 1p.m.?

Once we connect in person, the approach is the same, find out what their issues are, and leave with an action item. Are they struggling with building their referral business? Teach them this system! (And you'll be on their list... you'll be in their Tribe when they communicate with their Village!) Are they super busy but burning out because they don't have a good team? Refer them to a great business coach, buy them a book, or connect them with someone in their industry who's done a great job hiring people! There is no limit to how much value you can provide if you are just looking for ways to help people! For book recommendations, visit www.pursuingfreedom.co. I have a go-to set of great business books I like to recommend to my colleagues, depending on the issues they are dealing with.

What I've found over the years is that we get into a habit of referring one person, because it becomes our natural habit to do so. You'll see when you get into this kind of activity, it starts to come easily. Your friends and clients will start seeking you out for referrals because you'll become known as someone who's 'got a guy' for everything. My challenge to you would be to *seek out* folks to refer to who just "get it."

In other words, look to do business with and refer business to people who understand that intending to be a resource above and beyond the product or service you provide creates a circle of abundance and wealth not only for themselves but for everyone they come in contact with. It's important to refer to like-minded people. They tend to do a better job for your clients, and will likely be in business for the long run. Be careful not to refer your clients to folks who don't take their business seriously. This can be a tricky thing. You never want your name tied to a bad experience. But if you do your due diligence, and really get to know the people you're referring business to, you'll find this is an easy problem to avoid. And this is exactly why I recommend meeting with people in person and interviewing them before you add them to your referral directory.

I began to notice after the first few years of operating this way that there were folks in *my* Tribe that maybe didn't think of me as being in *their* Tribe, quite possibly because they'd never even thought of doing business this way. What I mean by that is I was referring business to them regularly, but not necessarily receiving referral business in return. So my challenge to you would be to make this a developing process. There's no end to what you can do with it. You start by getting into activity with the Village. You build a Tribe. You get to know them, and you continue to seek folks who are in alignment with how you do business, so you go from having one or two people singing your praises, to 30 or 40 Tribe members singing each other's praises! This is where the fun lies! And it may sound infeasible, but then I look back to where I started, referring a dentist who barely knew me from Adam, to referring a dentist who now treats my children, and has become a part of our family, and who has become a client, and a referral partner. It's a whole new world!

Whether you're just getting started or you already have a framework for this process, whether you're a natural connector or this doesn't come easily, there is limitless opportunity! You can start with a cursory list, but over time you must continually grow and refine that list until you feel connected with everyone in your Tribe, and they feel just as connected to you. Set at least one day per week, if not more, to work on this with intention, and watch the magic unfold!

As I mentioned, this is just the beginning! In the next chapter, we are going to explore the 'next steps.' How do we take this concept to the next level, and integrate it into a comprehensive marketing plan? This is not just a conversation, it's a strategy built on authenticity. We start with a sincere intention to help people, and then we develop an entire business plan around it. Get ready for the snowball effect. It's amazing!

CHAPTER 6

Marketing

At this stage of the game, you have a database of people you are trying to serve, who we call your Village. You have resources to serve them, your Tribe. And you're on purpose with your 'sales' calls, reaching out to connect with them and intend to be of value. Now what?

Well, before I get into the slew of things you can do with this community of people, I must first reiterate... picking up the phone is the most important thing you can do. I promise you, if you make 20 calls and follow the scripts provided, you will start seeing referrals coming in from areas you'd never imagine. If you wake up every day with the intention to help every person you encounter, you'll be rewarded tenfold. It's not complicated; it's simple. Pick up the phone and call every single person in your database, then call every single business owner you've been referred to, and THEN, read this chapter about additional ways to market yourself. This is supplemental to the basics of making phone calls.

Step 2 after making calls and setting appointments is the magical handwritten note. You've probably heard this before because it's pretty common sense. If you write 5 handwritten notes a day, you'll see your referral business explode. Now, when I was given this advice, I was all over it. I had no problem carving out time every day for notes, and found that it brought a number of rewards.

First off, when you set about your day, trying to decide who to write a note to, you'll run out of ideas pretty quickly. You really need to think outside the box to get 25 notes a week out the door. With hindsight, one of the results of this task was that I found myself listening better to everyone I spoke to. Whether I was on a call with a client, or in the doctor's office, or at a friend's house, I started intently listening for an opportunity to follow up with a note, a resource, and sometimes, my business card. If a friend was in need, I sent a note. I spoke to a client and heard they got a new job, I sent a note. The pediatrician was nice to my kid, I sent a note. I was a note-sending freak. And you know what? People appreciated it!

I started getting text messages, calls, and comments about the thoughtfulness of the notes, birthday cards, referrals, etc. Warm and fuzzy, yes, but from a strategic approach, guess what? People start thinking about you. A LOT of people are thinking about you, talking about you, and appreciating you. Like 100 people every month are thinking about you thinking about them! And you know what? They aren't talking about what a great salesperson you are. They are talking about what a thoughtful *person* you are! What's even better... it's FUN! I mean really, truly enjoyable. If this is work, it's the best job in the world. Don't get in your head about this. PEOPLE LIKE GETTTING PERSONAL CARDS IN THE MAIL. PERIOD. This is not rocket science.

I want you to open your mail for the next 5 days and see how many personal notes you get. If it's your birthday week, this doesn't count. But even then, how many handwritten notes are you even receiving for your birthday anymore? Don't get me wrong. It's nice to get 250 birthday messages on Facebook each year, but seeing a handwritten card in the mail is like a little treat. Why not be that treat in someone's day or week? Why not make everyone you meet feel special and important? It's a no brainer, and it's a game changer!

Step 3 is to communicate the fact that you have a referral directory at your fingertips and that you're actively and intentionally building it at all times, in order to be a resource to your friends and clients. If it's starting to sound like a broken record, it should. This should become your mantra. "My goal is to be your yellow pages." "My goal is to be a resource, above and beyond the product or service I'm selling." "I am building a referral directory of trusted local service providers to serve all your needs." "I've got a guy for that." Over and over and over, until everyone you meet knows you as the answer person. You should be saying these things so much, you're having dreams about it. Only once this becomes a habit, and sticks, will you start to see the results. And the results will be more than you ever dreamed imaginable!

Here are just a few ideas on how to take this concept to the next level. It's a limitless process

- **Create a monthly mailer**. Each month, you are going to interview a business owner in your Tribe, and include a blurb about them in your monthly mailer. The mailer is intended to connect your Village to your Tribe, and market yourself as a resource.

- In order to do this, you'll want to schedule a face to face meeting with the business owner, get a stack of their cards, one for every mailer you're sending. For some that may be 20, for some that may be 200. The number is less important than the action. I stopped including my own business card, because frankly, my Village knows how to reach me, and doesn't need 12 of my business cards each year. I put my photo and contact information on the letter, and included the business card of *someone else*, and I usually made it relevant to the time of year. An accountant in January, a florist in May, a roofer in July, a financial planner in December, you get the picture.

- Follow up. After the meeting, send a note to the business owner. Maybe you heard an action item in your meeting and can send a resource to help them? After the mailer goes out, make some calls to your Village. Ask them if they found your mailer helpful. Ask them if there's anything they need. Remind them "you've got a guy" for just about anything. I used to joke, "And if you need a mortgage, I've got a guy for that too. But I'm the guy."

- ○ If you connect on the phone with someone in your Village, send a note to follow up on the chat. Remind them to think of you if they need anything at all (including whatever product or service you offer.) A few weeks after the mailer goes out, follow up with the business owner. Find out if they received any calls from the mailer. Find out if there's anything going on in their life you can help with. Make a plan to catch up soon. Send another note if you've connected.

- **Create a tangible 'directory' to provide your clients.** I used to give business card holders at closing, filled with the business cards of the folks I know, like, and trust. I would tell them that if they didn't find the business card of someone they needed, to just call or text me, and I would find it. Because I have such a large Tribe, I can usually reach out to *them* for referrals when there's a gap in my directory. (Opens up opportunity for even more new relationships constantly!)

  - ○ I can't tell you how many random messages I've received from colleagues thanking me for referrals I didn't know I'd given, all because my clients looked in the little book for a business card. And I can't tell you how many mortgages I've done for those colleagues! This process has been so fun because along the way, I've organically trained my clients to think of me when they need anything. I receive text messages all the time asking for referrals of random service providers, and it instantly puts me on a mission.

o The answer is never, "No." The answer is either, "Yes, here you go," or, "Let me look into it and get back to you." Another great example, and an even simpler approach, is to simply print out a list on a Word document. I know an amazing property inspector who includes a sheet of paper in his inspection report with a list of service providers he trusts and refers to his clients. What an amazing value-add! Here's someone who's just inspected your home, and likely at a time that you may discover you need some services. Most folks do an inspection when they are selling or buying a home. If you're selling, you may be thinking of sprucing up the home with a new coat of paint, some landscaping, a professional carpet cleaning, etc. Or you may have items that need addressing, like plumbing, electrical or roof. His list was an instant value for the client. "Look no further, here are the folks I personally use and refer to my clients!" Love this.

○ In another marketing example, two sisters, both entrepreneurs in completely different fields (one is a licensed professional counselor and the other is a family photographer), created a magnet to send to their Village, with all of their favorite service providers and their contact information listed. They simply created a cool graphic, had it made into a large refrigerator magnet, and mailed it out to a couple hundred people. Then, they offered the magnet to their colleagues to send to *their* Villages. How genius is that? Anyone who wanted to provide this same value to their clients and friends could do so by simply purchasing the magnets (no profit to the creators). They provided value to their Tribe, value to their Village, and in doing so, they also marketed themselves by sharing the idea. Brilliant!

○ Another great idea is a visual display. My dentist has a plastic business card holder on the counter in her office, so patients can't help but browse the cards of her trusted colleagues as they check in for their dental appointment.

o   Another idea I saw was a stocked business card binder in an auto mechanic's waiting room. So as you're waiting for your car to be worked on, you peruse a book of trusted local business owners. This concept can be implemented in a number of industries, from health and wellness to automotive! The options are really limitless when it comes to tangibly promoting your Tribe to your Village!

- **Create an online directory**. Some folks don't have as much 'face time' with their clients as others. So many will opt to feature preferred service providers on their websites. When I created my blog www.pursuingfreedom.co my web designer suggested we take it a step further, and added a form for people to fill out if they are in need of a referral. That way, there's a call to action. I can see who needed the information and have the opportunity to follow up with them, as well as the service provider they were looking for. If we'd simply listed the contact information on the blog, it would be hard to track who we are helping. Either way you do it, you're promoting that intention to be of value, and this is your unique selling proposition!

- **Create video marketing for social media**. Set up filmed interviews of your Tribe members. Ask them to talk about what sets them apart from the competition, or inquire about how they built their business from the ground up. Highlight whatever it is that makes them special. Then give them the video to share on their social media sites... by default you'll be marketed to their Village now too!

  ○ I streamlined this process by setting up a 2-day video shoot with a professional videographer. We used an app called TimeTrade to let people schedule themselves. It was so easy. I simply sent an email to 25 people in my Tribe, inviting them to be interviewed for my blog, then provided the link to choose an open timeslot. Within 48 hours, I had 16 slots scheduled. Once the videos were complete, I then had 4 months of content for weekly blog posts, simply posting the videos to the blog, social media, etc., and asking the business owners to do the same. It's amazing how much more reach you have to connect with your Village when you're providing this kind of value!

o Some may wonder why I'd go to such lengths to market *other people*. Well, let's face it: nobody cares about mortgages unless they need one. And unless you're buying investment properties, you rarely need a mortgage more than every few years or so. And if you're like me, you probably think, "My clients don't want to hear from me after the sale because they already have what they need." This is the new conversation! This is the reason for being in touch. It's your purpose to provide *more value* than the product or service you're selling. And it's your guaranteed way of staying top of mind and receiving referrals from your clients!

- Some of you may read this and think it's easier said than done because of the line of work I'm in, but you'd be wrong to think you can't apply this to your business, regardless of the industry. Take my friends Jake Denham and Talia Kite. Jake is the owner of Jake's Carpet

Cleaning and Talia is the founder of Blissful Impressions, a newborn, wedding, and family photographer. Two amazing friends and entrepreneurs I've had the pleasure of working with and getting to know over the years. Jake and Talia wanted to provide value to their referral partners as well as their clients, so they collaborated to host a video interview series. Come to think of it, I guess I swiped this idea from them! They shared the videos with everyone they interviewed, and posted to social media, and increased their own exposure through video. Who would've thought a carpet cleaning company and family photographer would be able to reach their clientele in this manner? This approach is accessible to anyone willing to think outside the box!

- **Hold a client appreciation event, and invite your Tribe to attend**. Be the HUB of this network. The longer you do business this way, the more people will come to realize the value you bring to their lives. They will know that attending one of *your* events isn't like attending some average networking event. They know you will be connecting them with potential clients and referral partners because, heck, that's just what you do! It's amazing what relationships can blossom from these events! And it's fun!

- **Create a mastermind group with like-minded service providers**. Invite speakers to come talk about creating business plans, bookkeeping services, social media marketing, etc. Watch coaching videos. Share marketing ideas. Mastermind groups have been the foundation for many amazing friendships and business partners of mine over the years.

  o If you're not sure how to get started, here's an example. First, identify another industry that is also serving your target market or referral partner. For example, mortgage lenders try to connect with realtors as referral partners, because most homeowners call a realtor first, and the realtor refers the lender. Well, title companies also depend on referrals from realtors. (Many businesses benefit from referrals from realtors, so if you're a realtor, and can market yourself as a resource, this book's system is a great strategy for you!) So first start by partnering with a title company that intends to provide value to their clients and referral partners in the same way you do. Then, together, you can create an event to bring together like-minded business professionals in your target market.

- The benefit of going this route is twofold. First, you have a partner in crime, and an automatic accountability partner in this process. Second, you're now helping *each other* by exposing each other to your referral partners, who in turn may become friends and referral partners for one another.

  - I have a friend who's a builder, and he once told me about a builder services group he was a part of. So, on a larger scale, a number of business owners who benefit from referrals from builders created a group to provide value to builders. They meet monthly, and take turns featuring a few products or services that may be of value to the builders. They sponsor happy hours, ski trips, golf outings, etc., all in an effort to provide value, connect, and build relationships. If you're the only roofer in a group like this, who do you think the builders will think of when it's time to hire a roofing contractor? It's a no brainer! And again, it's a fun and authentic way to grow your business with like-minded professionals.

- You can even take this a step further and partner with business owners who are serving the same target market. For example, in doing my video interviews, I discovered that two massage therapists I know, as well as an acupuncturist, have long-term goals of opening a wellness center where clients will have access to a number of services under one roof. If you are in a business where you know your clients typically need other services that go hand in hand, collaborate with like-minded business owners in those complimentary fields. We see this a lot with real estate companies having an in-house mortgage lender. Or a chiropractor or personal trainer who has a massage therapist onsite. Regardless of your industry, the goal is the same: How can I provide *more* value??? If you ask yourself this on a daily basis, you'll be amazed by the ideas you can come up with!

- **Create a small accountability group**. This is a bit different than the mastermind group. It's smaller and more focused on the journey of the individual. Share your goals, your challenges, give and take advice, and become better friends. You have something major in common… your income is 100% commission, and as we've already established… this is really hard! Don't be an island in this journey.

This is a place to discuss and help one another with the hardest parts of this business, like work-life balance, team building, goal setting, business development, etc. It's amazing what happens when a few committed individuals work together to improve the lives of one another!

After joining a real estate mastermind group in September 2013, we broke off into small groups in December to share our goals and business plans for 2014. We committed to meeting monthly to hold each other accountable to our progress. As it turned out, it quickly became 'the most important meeting of the month' for the four of us. We started referring to it as 'real estate therapy.' We shared our goals, committed to monthly action steps, took notes, and followed up on our progress each month. Inevitably, we discussed and worked through our challenges. And it never had anything to do with the 'deals' we were working on. It was big picture stuff, and it was powerful. Even if you don't receive direct referrals from a group like this, don't underestimate the impact it has on your business. You leave inspired, and often with a clear mind on what you need to do to take your business to the next level. Oh yeah, and did I mention, it's FUN?!

- **Special Occasions**: Let's say one of your top referral partners or clients has a birthday, closes on a new house, or lands a new job. A handwritten note is a fantastic way to show you care. A little gift is even better. But what if you took it a step further? What if you thought outside the box and turned to your Tribe to find a unique gift? Maybe it's an overwhelmed working mom you're sending a gift to... how about a gift card to your favorite massage therapist? A client bought a new house? How about a gift card to the family photographer, who can take the first set of family photos in the new home? A working dad with a long 'honey-do' list? A gift card to for the handyman you know and like. The possibilities are limitless, and the impact is HUGE! You're showing someone you care, while providing value and potentially a client for life to one of your fellow Tribe members.

- ○ I've done this in waves. I had one colleague that was a professional outsourced personal assistant. For $30/hour, she would handle just about any personal or professional assistance. She'd pick your mom up from the airport, organize your closet, create a marketing mailer, manage your database, prep meals, you name it. What busy professional wouldn't benefit from a $100 gift card for 3+ hours of her services? This was such a fun and unique gift to give!

o Another gal I knew made custom gift baskets. I had some clients that were real estate investors. So between the 10 properties they own, I'd done so many purchases and refinances, I was out of creative gift ideas. So I contacted the gift basket company and let them know my clients liked beer and cooking. What she created for $150 was amazing! Rather than a traditional basket, the gift was packaged in a cooler. It included beer mugs, a beer bread mix, a cookbook with recipes made with beer, and a 12 pack of craft beers. It was so thoughtful and amazing! And all I had to do was write the check. The beautiful and creative gift was delivered to their door. The clients were amazed. And the best part was, besides giving a 'deal' to my colleague in the form of business, I connected her with another potential referral partner, as my clients are business owners too, and may find value using the custom gift basket company for their own clients. Always look for ways to connect people. It's such a fun way to do business!

CHAPTER 7

Plan for success

"Be ready when opportunity comes... Luck is when preparation and opportunity meet."
— Roy D. Chapin Jr.

If any of the content in this book resonates with you, this chapter may be the most important one you read, as it is where you prepare for your inevitable success. As we've already touched upon, if you set goals, identify the Village you want to serve, and wake up every day with the intention to give more value than you expect to receive in payment... YOU. CAN. NOT. FAIL. Simple as that. You cannot fail. Knowing this, please, please, please create a game plan to support your success.

Personally, I've experienced two types of overwhelming stress during my journey as an entrepreneur. One is the stress I felt when my bank account had the flu. Being broke is no fun. Well, sometimes it can be fun *going* broke, but *being* broke sucks. Waking up every day wondering how you're going to pay the bills, deciding what to say no to, or who to borrow from, is not fun. The burden is real. But you know what's amazing about being broke? There's so much opportunity! There's only one way to go, and it's up! And usually, if you're broke, it's because your business is slow, which means you have time on your hands. When you don't have a lot of clients, you have lots of time to get creative and get to work.

The other kind of stress is OVERWHELM. This is the kind of stress you need to prepare to avoid. Overwhelm is when you plug away, putting everything you've got into growing your business, and then you wake up one day and WHAM!!! Your business exploded overnight! It probably wasn't overnight, but it sure feels like it. You may be reading this right now and thinking, "I wish my business would explode," or, "I wish I was overwhelmed." Well, guess what? It's inevitable!!

And as crazy as it may sound, overwhelmed sucks almost as much as broke. Some days, even more. You know why? When you're not very busy, you have all the time in the world to love on people and give your clients the most amazing service experience they can imagine. You spend time with friends and family. You may exercise and eat slow meals. You're hungry for business, but you're energized. Why? Because you have *time*. When you only have one client, it's easy to take great care of them! When you only have one client, you can take a 1-hour hike in the mountains, or go golfing. You might be spending money you don't have, but in a weird way, it can still be liberating.

But when you reach the overwhelm stage, you've likely traded much of this time for more money. Yay! You probably start out maintaining that same level of service you set out to provide your clients. You begin to feel over-committed with friends and family, and find yourself working around the clock to stay caught up with your business. Before too long, you're saying no to friends and family, to golf and exercise, to your health. You work longer hours. You find yourself catching up on weekends, or before dawn, or late at night, or all of the above. You crave those quiet moments when your phone isn't ringing and nobody is firing back responses to your emails instantaneously. You drink more coffee.

You drink more wine! You sleep less. You're more irritable. And as this slowly but seemingly quickly becomes your normal, you just keep telling yourself to be grateful! You're so lucky to be this busy! And who knows how long it will last? So let's just keep plugging away. Our family sees how hard we're working so they quietly support us, even though they see the stress, and they feel it too.

My personal crash and burn came in the summer of 2012. In the first 5 years of my business, as I've mentioned, my business was growing organically, slow and steady. It had become stable and reliable, but never overwhelming. Then, during 2010 and 2011, I'd begun to take my business more seriously. I'd become tired of being broke, and started getting serious about applying the principles I was learning from my business coach, the books, and the seminars. I worked really hard in 2011 to put systems in place for success, and guess what? It worked! In 2012, my business more than doubled. I went from averaging 35 transactions a year for the previous 3 years to doing nearly 80 in 2012. I was pregnant with my second child. I had no 'assistant' at the office. My husband was working long hours as a teacher. And I was on the verge of a nervous breakdown.

Here I was having my best year ever, but I was struggling. And I looked at my colleagues, who were doing even more volume than I was, also without help. They admitted to staying at the office until midnight or going home to see their kids at 5 p.m., only to tuck them in at 8 p.m. and work in their home office until the crack of dawn. If I was burning out, how do you think they felt? I was picking my 2-year-old up at daycare, shoving some microwaved mac-n-cheese in his mouth, and calling it good. I was a shell of myself. And I was a pretty shitty wife, mother, and friend. I was desperate for an escape. How could I possibly want to *grow* my business anymore? If my life looked like this, and my colleagues' lives looked like they did, what on earth was I aspiring to?

So you know what I did? I tried to start a skincare business as my escape plan. Yup. With all my free time, I figured, why not *add* to it? Genius, Erin. I mean, how could this not work out? But you know what? I was desperate. I was exhausted. My debt was paid off and we had money in the bank, and I was miserable. I was about to have my second child, and I was looking forward to maternity leave like some kind of sick vacation. Thank God for my sweet and supportive husband. I convinced him that I could make the skincare business work (and I still believe I could, but not while running a mortgage business with no help, and a second baby on the way!).

He stood by as I invested in another business, and spent even *more* time out of the house trying to build the business. I literally wore my 4-week-old in a wrap on my chest, as I gave presentations on skincare. My husband was supportive, but my girlfriends tried to have an intervention. They were worried about me. If you've ever known an entrepreneur whose business is succeeding, but they are a one-man show, you know what I'm talking about. Everyone around you can see you're running at a breakneck pace, and probably doing damage to your health and your family, but you just keep pushing because you don't know any other way. Heck, you have to remind yourself to be *grateful* to be so busy!

Guess how that worked out for me? Total self-sabotage. First and foremost, after taking an oar out of the water with my mortgage business while I enjoyed my 'vacation,' or maternity leave, my business took a big dip. Meanwhile, I'd invested what little savings we'd finally built up into the skincare business, and then some. Next thing I knew, it was the end of 2013, and we were deep in debt again.

Here's the deal. I tell you this story to help you. Please don't follow in my footsteps. I wasn't very smart. I was daring, but dumb! I built a successful business to the point of overwhelm, and hated being overwhelmed so much, I ran from the success. I shrunk my vision and started thinking small. I started telling myself, "We only need so much money to survive." "I don't need to work this hard." "It's not worth it." The problem is, as human beings, we are wired for progress. There's a saying, "If you're not growing, you're dying." There are studies that show the parallel between the decline in your contribution to society and your physical health. We need to be growing. Shrinking is depressing and not fulfilling. Don't follow my path! Don't shrink when the business gets going. GROW.

This chapter was titled 'Plan for Success' for a reason. And here's the bottom line. Don't go it alone. Planning for success means planning to have support in place. Expecting to grow means expecting to hire. I tried going it alone for 8 years, and now you know how that worked out for me. In 2014, I finally hired a team member. She happened to be one of my best friends, so it not only helped my business, it made it more fun! I know that sounds like a huge no-no to most folks, but for me, sharing the journey with people I love has made the process all the more enjoyable.

As I mentioned, I was broke at the end of 2013. I was determined to succeed (again), but this time, I was determined to do it better. I refused to accept the 'one-man show' that is so prevalent in the real estate industry. I refused to believe that the only way to stay out of debt and build our savings was to work 12-hour days and be on call 7 days a week. I was convinced there had to be another way. So I planned to hire my first team member by June, 2014. In order to do so, I set some production goals that would justify and support bringing on an employee.

Now, if you're reading this and sitting on a bunch of credit card debt, you may be thinking "I can't afford to hire help." Well, guess what, you can't afford not to. The best business coach I've ever had always says, "Your next closing is not as important as your next hire, because your next hire is your next 100 closings." And he is spot on. How to hire, when to hire, and who to hire is another book in itself, so rather than go there, I'll just recommend one that's already been written. It may just change your life forever. Read *The E-Myth Revisited*, by Michael Gerber. It's an amazing book that will give you a step by step approach to planning for success and building your team. I wish someone had given it to me 10 years ago. It would have radically changed the speed and trajectory of my career. It will change the way you think about your business. It will take your ego out of the equation and mitigate your fear of growth and overwhelm. It's an absolute essential read for anyone who wants to take their business seriously, and take it to the highest level imaginable.

And if you're reading this and happen to be in the mortgage industry, like me, you'll need to call the Mortgage Marketing Animals. I hired Carl White and his team in late 2015, and owe much of my happiness to them. They've helped me realize that being a one man band is no way to live. Our growth doesn't have to come to a halt the moment we realize we have no more minutes in a day to contribute to our career. Our mission should be to regularly and systematically leverage our time and resources to create a stable and thriving business. I absolutely love the way they've managed to change my perspective and help me remove obstacles on the journey to success. And my family appreciates them even more!

Whatever happens, *expect* huge success, and plan accordingly. You've got nothing to lose!

CHAPTER 8

The Nuts and Bolts

As we come to an end here, I hope you are fired up and ready to take action! You've accepted the fact that your business won't grow if you don't figure out how to promote your value. You've got a plan, a message, and a script to get your message out there. You've identified your Village and you're on your way to building your Tribe to serve them. As Dr. Seuss would say, "Today is your day!"

In case you haven't figured it out yet, I'm a little bit passionate about the journey and success of the entrepreneur. I love dare devils, risk takers, and lovers of life! We see an opportunity and we jump in with both feet. We CREATE opportunities! And we struggle. We doubt. We fear just as much as anyone else. So my number one take away for you is this: Do not go it alone. Everything about this journey is about community.

Build a community of people to serve. *Design* your database of clients. Then build another community of like-minded service providers to help you take great care of your people. Handpick a Tribe of amazing entrepreneurs. Create a Village of supporters! Seek out friends to ride alongside you on the journey, to share your goals, your challenges, and your successes. Hire a coach to help you overcome your fear and self-doubt. Then build an amazing team to enable you to impact the lives of more and more people! Hire people you love and treat them well. Build a community of people who love their job and love their boss! Do not go it alone!

Fill your brain with positivity. Devour books. Hire a coach. Attend seminars. Join a mastermind group. Create a mastermind group! The biggest recipe for failure is trying to succeed as an island. It's absolutely impossible to succeed without the help of MANY people.

Plan for success. You cannot fail! You're not alone. Whether you're broke or overwhelmed, do not give up. Revise, rework and keep on going. Believe it's possible, and enjoy the journey. Freedom awaits!

Will you succeed? Yes you will indeed!
Ninety-eight and three-quarters
percent guaranteed

Dr. Seuss

About the Author

Hi. I'm Erin Bradley. I'm a mortgage consultant, speaker, coach, and lover of all things entrepreneur. I wrote this book because I want to help you overcome the fear of sales and make your business awesome. In 2006, after a few years of travel and adventure, I fell into working for a mortgage company. It didn't take long for me to realize I liked working for myself and didn't want a boss. But it took *forever* to figure out how to make any money! Since then, I developed a unique and replicable system that has helped me, and countless others, overcome the fear of sales and build a successful referral business.

In 2015, I was featured in Top Agent Magazine and Mortgage Executive Magazine as one of the top 1% of Mortgage Originators nationwide. I've been named 5 Star Mortgage Professional by Denver's 5280 Magazine every year since 2014. But none of this matters if I'm not having fun and helping others! Over the years, I built a network of local service providers and became obsessed with the disconnect between doing what you love and financial freedom. I devoured sales books, hired coaches, and finally developed a strategy that would allow me to grow my business by referral, in a way that's truly authentic and fun. My business and life have never been the same! It wasn't long before I started teaching others how to do the same, and discovered that this system is transferable to other industries.

My mission in life is to help entrepreneurs achieve success and freedom as fast as possible. When I'm not working, I'm hanging out with my awesome husband Tony, and our hilarious kids, Mickey and Jo Jo, in sunny Colorado. Living the dream and hoping to help you do the same!

A Year in Review and a Better Future for You!

———◇———

Better results start with a plan. Many of these resources were shared with me in 2011, and came from a website called www.MakingBetterHappen.com I've since tweaked the process to better fit my needs, and this is the resulting system I've used over the past few years to set goals, create a business/life plan, and see consistent and predictable GROWTH! I hope it helps you as it's helped me!

Grab a pen and paper and start free writing, using these questions as your guide:

1. What are the 5 of Greatest Happenings of the last year?
2. What are 3 new things I learned or did in the last year?
3. What 3 new relationships did I develop in the last year?
4. What 3 existing relationships did I deepen in the last year?
5. Have I been persistent in following through on my plans?
6. If I could go back and do it again, what are 3 things I would've done differently?
7. What books did I read in the last year?
8. Is there someone I need to contact and thank?
9. Is there someone I need to contact and make amends to?
10. What's the biggest risk taken in the last year, and if none, what held me back?
11. What's the smartest decision I made in the last year?
12. What's one word that sums up the last year?
13. What do I need to KEEP doing in the next year?
14. What do I need to START doing?
15. What do I need to STOP doing?

16. 3 great things about my home and where I live are:

17. 3 great things about where I work and what I do for a living are:

18. 3 great gifts of unique talent and skill I've been given are:

19. Am I missing anything in my life that's important to me?

20. What is it about my career that makes me feel trapped?

21. What realistic changes can I make in how I run my business to experience more freedom?

22. What must I personally do that cannot be delegated to anyone else?

23. Am I living a balanced life?

24. How much money is enough, and if I have more than enough, what am I doing with the excess?

3 WORDS: choose 3 words that represent your goals

for the next year. These words can represent the mindset it will take to achieve them, the environment, the mood, etc. The words should give you a huge picture, not a small one. Some of the words I've used are Receive, Abundance, Teach, Delegate, Ask, Process, Breathe, Balance, Inspire, etc.

VISION: Map out your vision for your life and business. By this time next year, I am _____, I have _____, I will _____, etc. Questions to you ask yourself:

- What type of clients do I want?
- Who will support me?
- Who are my ideal colleagues and referral partners?
- Why do people work with me?
- What sets me apart from the rest?
- What do people say about me?
- How do I treat my clients and team members?

GOALS:

Now, take a few minutes to write out some specific goals in the following areas, using these **Thought Starters** to help you:

Business: grow purchase business, build a team, recruiting, brand reputation, customer satisfaction, new skills, find a mentor, mentor someone else, etc. (No filter on this!)

Financial: income, savings, total net worth, begin investing, pay off debt, buy a home, save for college, set up trust/estate, etc.

Physical: ideal weight, run marathon, increase flexibility, elevate energy, reduce cholesterol, start meditating, go to bed earlier/wake earlier, etc.

Mental: read 30 minutes a day, listen to educational podcasts, go to seminars, hire a coach, build new skills, etc

Family: spend more time with family, be home for dinner every night, read to my kids every night, date night with spouse once a week, visit parents twice a year, forgive or make amends with a relative, attract Mr. or Mrs. Right, plan vacations with family, etc

Lifestyle: travel, adventure, luxuries, languages, hobbies, instruments, where you want to live, how you want to live, how you want your home, who you want to meet, etc.

Now, you should have a few pages of notes. Take out a pen or highlighter, and read through the pages, and identify the actionable items. This will help you identify your goals, values and mission for the next year!

Specific goals could include:

- Total volume/sales for the year
- Average sales price
- Number of units (listings/purchases)
- Number of meetings with A+ referral partners per week
- What behaviors/actions do I need to have on a daily/weekly basis?

TOP TEN GOALS: from the notes, identify your top ten goals for the next year.

And from the top ten, identify your **TOP 3 GOALS:**

1. _____

2. _____

3. _____

2015 Simple Business Plan

TOP 10 GOALS

1. 10 Loans Per Month
2. Become an HBM expert
3. Buy another property
4. Hire Processor and LOA
5. Read 12 books
6. 2 notes per day
7. Visit Family in PHL and FL.
8. Kids activities- ride a bike, soccer, etc
9. 6 camping weekends
10. Weekly Massage

BANNER GOALS

1. 30M volume or 10 units/mo
2. Buy another property
3. Build Team

3 WORDS
DELEGATE
TEACH
RECEIVE

Schedule

Mon:	8a-9a: 5 NOTES
	9a-10a: call backs
	10a-11a: team meeting
	2p: 3 focus calls
Tues:	11:30-end of biz: mtgs
Wed:	8a-9a: 5 NOTES
	9a-10a: HBM
	2p: 3 focus calls
Thur:	8a-noon: meetings
	2p: 3 focus calls
Friday:	8a-9a: create call list
	9a-10a: database
	Delegate lender letters!

ROCKS IN MY SCHEDULE

Weekly team meeting
- 10 thank you notes or gifts
- BNI
- min 2 mtgs with ambassadors
- visit database/track/CRM

Monthly Rainmakers
- Accountability group
- Buffini Mastermind
- Realtor or Financial Planner Class
- Girls night out: Mar - Jun - Sep - Dec
- Advocate appreciation: Feb

89

BUILD YOUR TRIBE

Accountant	
Accupuncture	
Attorney (BK, Family, Etc)	
Mechanic	
Auto Broker	
Personal Banker	
House Cleaner	
Carpet Cleaner	
Flooring Specialist	
Chiropractor	
Photographer	
General Contractor	
Dentist	
Pediatrician	
Electrician	
Financial Planner	
Wedding Planner	
Florist	
Inspector	
Insurane (home, life, etc)	
Interior Designer	
Landscaper	
Massage Therapist	
Mortgage Consultant	
Moving Company	
Optometrist	
Personal Trainer	
Physical Therapist	
Plumber	
Roofing Contractor	
Handyman	
Window Cleaner	
Estate Planner	

Acknowledgments

My heart explodes with gratitude every day for the people I've been so lucky to know. First, to my husband Tony. To call him supportive would be an enormous understatement. None of my success would have been possible without his endless encouragement, belief, and partnership in insanity! Thank you for lighting up my life with your awesomeness and humor Tony.

To my perfect little maniacs, Mickey and Jo Jo, my 'why.' Everything I've ever done was in anticipation of your arrival, and my hope to spend as much time with you as possible. Thank you for being my adventure buddies! So much fun awaits us.

To my amazing parents, Mary Ann and Michael Foley, to whom I owe the deepest gratitude for instilling in me the belief that anything is possible. The life and education you provided me empowered me to go after any dream, and I've dreamt big because of you. Thank you for showing me what business ethics, drive, and perseverance looks like.

To my siblings, Patrick, Molly, Shannon, and Ryan, (and our amazing Outlaws!) for giving me a sense of humor. Life shouldn't be taken too seriously. I never laugh harder than when I'm with you!

To my 'work wives,' Jennifer Corwin, Molly O'Hagan, Rachael Kommer, Brooke Kelsey and Ginger Alferos, for taking the leap of faith and hopping onboard the crazy train. How lucky am I to work with my best friends?! My life was forever changed when you joined the team. The future is bright!

To my business buddy and original partner in crime, Euan Graham, for the never-ending book recommendations, advice, friendship and support. This journey wouldn't have been possible without you! Thanks for not letting me quit the business to be your office manager. Ha!

And to our accountability partners, Justin Knoll and Ryan Conover, for our two years of "real estate therapy." Your insights and encouragement inspired me and undoubtedly helped me take my business and life to new levels. You're part of the reason I wrote this book. I appreciate you guys so much!

To the O.G., Jeff Webb, who's been with me since the beginning. You've taught me so much about business and entrepreneurship, and helped my family on the road to financial freedom. Plus, you're really fun. I appreciate you more than you'll ever know!

To my mastermind crew, Lindsey Benton, Sima Patel, and Sean and Molly Hollis, for being downright awesome! Your friendship has helped me stay the course, and your commitment to personal and professional development has been an inspiration. In other words, you ROCK.

And to all my amazing realtor partners in crime, Jane Goulder, Bret Weinstein, Katie Turner , Sara Wilhelm... too many to name... thank you! We feel so blessed to be on your short list, and so lucky we get to do business with friends. All the coffees and lunches (and wine!) have been integral to surviving this crazy ride. Thanks for letting me on your bus!

To Brian Buffini, though we haven't met yet, and the numerous coaches that helped pull me out of the trenches. Your program was the catalyst. You continue to inspire me and countless others who are lucky enough to have discovered you. Thank you from the bottom of my heart.

To my coaches, Carl White and Tammy Conley, and the rest of the Freedom Club, for helping me create the life of my dreams. I don't know how I found you, but I'm sure glad I did. My life is forever changed because of you magical unicorns, and my family thanks you!

To my cousin Alicia, for being my pen pal when we were little. I bet it's thanks to you I grew up to write a book one day. Thanks for being 'my favorite.' (How do you know?) You're the best travel buddy and Rummy 500 player I've ever known.

To my girlfriends, near and far, my BC roomies, my Denver Village, the O.M.G., and my childhood homies, you know who you are! Thank you for keeping me sane and for making me laugh so hard I wet my pants. It sure does take a village!

I love you all more than words can express. My life is amazing and my heart is full because of YOU (and many, many more I've probably failed to mention!). I hope you know how much I appreciate you.

65490851R00053

Made in the USA
Middletown, DE
27 February 2018